Mary Paxson
Her Book

MARY PAXSON

Her Book

1880–1884

With an Introduction by
AGNES SLIGH TURNBULL

Illustrated by
PELAGIE DOANE

Applewood Books
Bedford, Massachusetts

Thank you for purchasing an Applewood Book.
Applewood reprints America's lively classics—books
from the past that are still of interest to modern readers.
For a free copy of our current catalog, write to:
Applewood Books, P.O. Box 365, Bedford, MA 01730.

ISBN 1-55709-582-5

Library of Congress Control Number: 2001095342

10 9 8 7 6 5 4 3 2 1

INTRODUCTION

ONCE in a long time an authentic bit of child-hood is captured and held within the pages of a book, so that other children in spirit, whether old or young, may enjoy it. Such a book is Mary Paxson's. The real diary of a real little girl in the early 80's, it has the sweetness, charm, and inimitable humor of *unconscious* literature in its rarest form.

From the time the young author reports the caterpillar as "the smallest fur-bearing animal," and describes her habit of saving the oyster's "stummicks" for Timothy Ticklepitcher, the cat, we are enchanted. And this delight grows through the pages. There is, indeed, something almost nostalgic in the picture of two little girls sewing their patchwork while their mother reads Enoch Arden aloud to them!

Mary Paxson's book is one to keep on a near-by shelf to read when life seems hurried and nerve-racking. For here is a breath of sweetness and ordered living from a past day, freshly preserved for us in this little diary!

AGNES SLIGH TURNBULL

1880

Diary January 1 1880

i asked papa if i could have this book and keep a
Diary in it and he said yes if i would not forget to
write in it, i am very busey most of the time but
will try and remember and another thing i musent
forget to brush my teeth 2 times every day without being told, it seems queer to make 1880 after
making 1879 so long mamma says it will be nice
for me to know when ime grone up what i did
when i was little, i dont do much but go to school
and wipe dishes and play with Maggie and myself
for Maggie would rather read than play, i wouldent, we have to go to school tomorrow after a
holliday week i am 7 years old, i went to school
when i was 5 years old and i have been going ever
since only when i have sore throtes

January 7, 1880, it is very cold, Maggie and i went
on the hill back of our house with our sleds and
coasted after school was out, Timmy has a cold
he is our cat and his real name is Timmothy
Ticklepitcher but it takes to long to say all that

so we just call him Timmy he is 1 year older than
i am, we had fried oysters for suppir i dont like
to eat there stummicks so i saved all the stummicks for Timmy he likes them very much,

January 15 1880 i got laughed at in school today
and i dident like it, the teacher asked me what is the
smallest fur berring annimal and i said a catterpiller and i ought to say a mouse and i dont care
a catterpiller is littler than a mouse and it has fur
on it,

January 16, 1880 mamma says i mustent forget to
make cappital eyes when I mean me I guess I wont
forget any more

January 24, I dont do much to write about it is
saterday afternoon and mamma says Maggie and
I can go out with our sleds after we both of us
make a patch work block, Maggie has to sew 1 on
saterdays and so do i, i have an inch more to sew
in my block than Maggie has, I masured them,
my seems make 15 inches to sew and Maggies
seems make 14 inches, our blocks arent alike thats
why,

February 7, 1880, I wouldent know how to spell the
Months if I dident copy it out of the callender,

i have an inch more to sew in my
block than Maggie has, I masured them,
our blocks arent alike thats why,

Maggie and I went to the librerry and we got little women to read we love the books that Louisa Alcott makes and Mamma is going to read it to us while we hem a towel and sew our patch work, I made my doll a pretty cote this morning, when I am grone up I am going to make books like Louisa Alcott does

February 21, 1880, I am 8 years old today mamma gave me a book and that is the most I got Maggie gave me a bottle of colone and papa gave me a little pocket book with 25 cents in it, that is the most money I ever had all at once before

February 22 and it is George Washingdons birthday and its another holliday that came on sundy instead of on a school day and we always get cheeted when hollidays come on saterdays and sundys, and if he was living he would be 148 years old I substrackted it myself sos I would know, tomorrow at school we all must tell something about him and I am going to say that he road a big white horse to war named Blueskin, I have a pitcher of it, it came with my paper Childrens Home Companion and Maggie takes the Youthes Companion but we both read each others papers,

the teacher said to find out some little thing inter-
ressting so I thought about his horse would do,

February 29, 1880 this month makes it leap year
because it has to have an extra day to make things
come out even evrey 4 years thats why

March 9, 1880, mamma says I have plenty of room
in my diary and for me not to croud my writing up
so much so I wont, there was a candy horse at the
store and I wanted it and it cost 10 cents and
looked awful good papa said I might buy it if I
saved my money and I musent take any out of my
bank its against rules to take money out of our
banks only to count it and put it right back, I take
mine out very often to count and I have lots, it was
43 cents the last time I counted it. it took me 2
weeks to save 10 cents sos I could buy my horse
and I went to the store today to buy it and some
boddy had bought it first, I felt very bad and so
did Maggie but I bought sourballs instead I never
had so many sourballs all at once before, I got
10 and gave Maggie 5 and we were going to have
a splendid time sucking them but we dident have,
we came home with 1 in each of our cheeks and
mamma made us take them out and she cracked
them in 2, we arent ever alloud to suck a whole

March 21, 1880, I let a little mouse
out of the trap today nobody saw me
do it,

sourball, mamma says it looks very unladylike
to bulge our faces out that way but we dident
mind a bit, I wish I had my 10 cents back, I never
wrote so much in my Diary before,

uncle Tommy Smith and he isent my rele uncle
was burried today he made our dolly beds and
mammas lap bord, Papa told me to rite that
uncle Tommy Smith father shot the last wolf
in bucks county in 1796

March 14, 1880, it is sundy and we went to meeting
and first day school, we dont go to church and
sundy school like Lizzie Auld and Ella Hays do
for we are Quakers thats why

March 21, 1880, I let a little mouse out of the trap
today noboddy saw me do it,

March 24, 1880, I have 2 things to put in my Diary,
grandmother Scarborough died, last 7th day and
it seems terrible, she is the only one I ever knew
that died, we didnt want it to happen, and Lon
got married today to Hellen Briggs and Maggie and
I didnt want him to get married and go way from
home, Mamma says he will live with Hellen Briggs
now and wont live with us any more its terrible,

April 3, 1880, it is nice and warm out doors and
we swung til we got tired then we jumpped rope

til we got out of breth and then we made stilts,
Maggie made a pair out of bean poles but they were
so rikkerty we couldent walk on walk on them so we
found 2 pales that were loose in the back fence and
we took them and 2 that werent loose and made
nice stilts and we can walk on them real well, we
had a splendid time,

April 29, 1880 Mamma read Claras amusements
out loud to us while we made our patch work
blocks, one of mammas teachers gave it to her
when she was just as old as I am now it says so in
the front of the book and it says reward of merit
and we dont get them at our school, and it says
to my little friend from her teacher Susanna Ely
and she married papas uncle David and now she
isnt mammas teacher but is our Aunt Sue Small
and lives at Oconomowoc wisconsin thats why, I
have to study my lessons for mondy my mental
arithametic is hard, I get to thinking about some
other things and then I forget and I miss most
evrey day, papa says theres no doubt that mental
arithametic is my waterlou and Ile understand
better what that is when Ime grone up,

May 1, 1880, our school went maying, today,
another holliday we got cheeted out of because it

we always get pretty well scratched
and torn when we go Maying

came on a saterday, we went to Fleecy Dale and
caleb Evans said it is named Fleecy Dale because
a mill that cardid fleece used to do it there. He
said fleece is the same as wool, and cardid is making
it nice like combing it would, and I was May
queen because I am the littelest girl and when
I got home I put my wreath in the wash basin and
we got lots of flowers our baskets just full and
birch and our handkychiefs full of tea berries and
we ate them for supper with sugar and cream on
them and we made willow wissles and I had to
make 3 before any would wissle right and I tore
my dress and we climed up the indian path to the
cave and Maggie found an arra head and we had a
splendid time, mamma said we looked more like
wild gipsies than like little girls when we got home
we always get pretty well scratched and torn when
we go Maying ny legs are awful tired tonight and
so are Maggies legs,

May 16, 1880, yesterday was saterdy and we had
the best time we ever had before, mamma took
Maggie and me to Philladelphia to get some new
coats and dresses and things and we had a good
dinner and then we had a splendid time, mamma
took us to the matinee, I asked her how to spell it

right, it is what happens in a house named a theater and we had never been before in all our lives but mamma had, and it was beautyfull and it was an opera named Iolanthe and an opera is where they sing, I dont know as if I ever had quite such a good time before and Maggie dont either, it was all nice but the nicest on top of all was going to the matinee,

May 17, 1880, Uncle Jene and Aunt Pattie burried their twin babies today, they had 2 of them and when people have 2 they make twins, There names were called Ruth and Watson after mamma and papa, Mamma gave them their close and got the little coffen and the babies were called Ruth and Watson, I wish we had 2 twins but not dead ones, mamma says she doesnt wish so, she says she is sattisfide with 2 that she has and no more,

June 12, 1880, mamma says I must try to puncher-ate my writing better than I do, I put commas where perriods belong. perriods always belong at the end and once in awhile before you get to the end. we had strawberries for supper tonight, Maggie and I picked them.

June 18, 1880, It is friday and school is out because it is vacation thats why and I wont have any more mental arithametic to bother me and spoil all my good times for all of vacation, we have to take naps though and they are about as bad, we always have to take naps when vacation comes, it takes lots of time, we wish mamma would forget about naps but she always remembres. Maggie and I went fishing today and we got our feet soking wet, we dident catch any fish only 1 bull frog and we dident know what to do with it. so we cut the line, and it was an awful wicked thing to do to let it go with the fish hook fast in its stummick. we were afraid to take it off of the hook. Maggie said it was my bull frog because I caught it and I said it was her bull frog because she told me to dangel the worm in front of it to see what it would do and before we knew it the bull frog grabbed the worm and swalled it and the hook to, I wish we hadent been so wicked and crule.

July 4, 1880, A good many years ago and I wasent born yet some men made a declaration of Independence, I copied how to spell it, and they put there names to it, a lot of them did and there was a big time and war and lots of things and mamma and papa werent born yet nor Maggie either, It was before our time thats why. and today is a holliday and always will be forever I wish 4th of July came in winter when there is school but it would always come on a saterday or a sundy if it did. we put 4 flags out on the front porch that we keep on purpose to cellebrate with, one on each porch post and we spent the day at Grandpa Paxsons and Grandmas and this evening we had some fire works not near enough though.

July 15, 1880, Maggie and I have been playing opera only we cant sing much or make our dolls sing either, mamma says when little girls havent tallents they must make tallents out of the plain things and wiping dishes is the plainest things I know how to do and I dont believe I can make many tallents out of doing that.

August 18, 1880, papa is 39 years old today and it is his Birthday and he is pretty old. there isent much to write about, we help mamma and sew a block of patch work evrey day, and none on saterdays, and we take naps evrey afternoon only we would rather not. I havent had a good time today because I had to go to the Dentist and have 3 teeth filled, the things I don't like is going to the Dentist and mental arithametic and naps, the things I do like is good times and cats and dolls and going to the matinee.

August 30, one day more than a week ago Rachie Preston and I went to the woods and took our dolls and made a play house and played all the afternoon and the next day I was awfelly poisoned, my hands and face and arms and neck and eyes and ears and fingers and I itched for a week worse than I ever itched all together before, hives and evreything, and I couldent see for it made my eyes shut and the Doctor said it was shoe mack poison and it wouldent be quite so bad if I had got poisoned next week after school begins but it was mean to take a hole week out of my vacation to get poisoned in.

September 18, 1880. We have been going to school 2 weeks and I have learned a lot. My dates must have perriods and not commas after them and I must use more cappitols when I begin to say things and always make a perriod at the end and commas in the middle. Mamma says I spell many words wrong and if I knew which ones Ide fix them right. Mamma says after we get washed and clean close on we may go to the librerry and get a fresh book to read, we read lots of books.

October 7, 1880. It is Maggies Birthday and she is 10 years old and she is fat and I am lean.

October 15, 1880 I had to put in a nother page because I forgot to write that my grate uncle and my grate aunt came to visit us, they are Aunt Susanna and Uncle David and they live in oconomowoc, I asked papa how to spell it. I like them very much and so do Mamma and papa like them, he is my grandmother Paxsons brother, I havent any, and oconomowoc is a place in wisconsin a grate way off, and Mr. George Lere is a lowyer and my Uncle David is to and he showed my uncle how and he came to our house to see my uncle David I have a lot of grate uncles and aunts and so has Maggie and we both have lots and piles of ones that arent grate just plain ones. I had to wipe dishes for our girl tonight, Mamma says its the only way to learn how and I dont care if I dont learn how. Mamma took us to the millinaries today and bought us 2 new hats and now we have new best hats we are to ware our hats that were best for evrey day ones. We used our best blue finger boles when we had company the day Mr Lere ate dinner at our house.

October 16, 1880. It is Sunday and I have spelled it wrong ever since I could spell and enny way I

I had my red dress on and the
geese and old gander got after me
and I screamed and yelled

oughent say them that way for we are Quakers
and Quakers say First Day and just like that only
1 more added to it all through the week like this,
thats why Second Day Third Day Forth Day
Fifth Day Sixth Day Seventh Day First Day,
We went down to grandpas and Maggie and I
both picked a quart of chestnuts and grandpa
gave us both a big lot more. I had my red dress
on and the geese and old gander got after me and
I screemed and yelled.

November 3, 1880. Papa and Mamma went to
Dellaware to see Cousin Ellen Good married,
Maggie and I didnt go because we were not asked.
Cousin Ellen is Aunt Anns Daughter and they
live in Wilmington, it has been a good while since
school opened, I wish Christmas was here

November 25. It is Thanksgiving Day and Papa
says I must write and tell about the Election,
James A Garfield is Elected president. Hayes is
our president now, but when next March comes
Garfield has to be If I wasent only 8 years old
and a girl Ide help vote to. I do vote at school for
we do that way to settle things sometimes. Papa
says to write the new sensus is 50 millions and he
said some more but I forget only it wasent enough

left over to make 51 millions of people yet so I
wont bother. Papa says Garfield is an able man,
and Chester A Author is Vice president. We are
most all repubblicans at school and our teacher is
a repubblican to and he votes and we raised a pole
and a flag and cheered til we got horse. It is
snowing and sleighs are running. We had terrible
happenings at school yesterday, Charlie Black
said Ile be darned if I will when the teacher said
for him to stay in at recess and he said it right out
loud and the teacher sent him to the woods to cut a
hickery stick to be whipped with and the stick
broke because it was cut half way across sos it
would brake and then the teacher sent another
boy for another stick to whip with. I don't like
such terrible happenings, Mamma says if she was
me she wouldent write about such things. It isent
nice to say such things like Charlie Black did only
I don't ever say them and Maggie doesent either.

November 27, and its Saturday and my Mother is
38 years old and today is her Birthday. Maggie
gave her a pen wiper and a holder and I gave her
a pincuchion and we made them all ourselves and
Mamma dident know it. Papa gave her a book.
We have been playing in the snow and we made

It is Christmas and its another Holliday
that dident come on a school day.
They dont any Hollidays ever come
only on Saturdays and Sundays

a long row of snow men and they were the Ennemy
and then we made a great big pile of snow balls and
a fort and we banged the Ennemy all to pieces
and there wasent any thing left but a few pieces
of arms and legs and things when we got done
banging.

December 25, 1880. It is Christmas and its another
Holliday that dident come on a school day. They
dont any Hollidays ever come any more only on
Saturdays and Sundays and they are Hollidays
anyway. We went to Uncle Quimbys to dinner
and had lots of good things to eat. Maggie and I
have a beautifull Christmas tree and lots of nice
things. I read some of my new book The Little
Mother and her Christmas. Ime glad we arent so
poor like they are and Ime glad my Mother is
home and not away sick in a hospittle like there
Mother is. I have lots of candy and nuts and lots
of things but not enough dolls.

1881

January 1. 1881. Its a new year and its been a good while since a year ago, my book isent near full and will be enough for another year. Today is New Years Day because it commences 1881 thats why, and its another Holliday to come on a Saturday.

February 1. 1881, and it is a hard month to spell and my birthday comes in it only not for a terrible long time yet. Papa says I will never need a new Diary if I keep writing at this rate. I just do the same things evrey day. I get up and I wipe the brekfast dishes and Maggie makes our bed and we go to school at 8 oclock and dont get back home til $\frac{1}{2}$ past 4 and then play some and set the supper table and take turns wiping supper dishes and I have to go to bed at 8 oclock but Maggie can stay up till $\frac{1}{2}$ past 8 because she is older thats why. I like to go to school and I like to help Mamma, and we study our lessons after supper and I like all my lessons but mental arithametic. I like my dolls only I havent any real nice ones any more. I have only five and there is something the matter with all of them. I want a new one terribly bad but Mamma says I must be patient, thats what you have to wait for til your Mothers and your Fathers get ready.

February 11, 1881. Papa vissited our school today, he is a school Directer, I am glad he is for he can say no. He said it about any more whippings.

I am learning history and literature at school now and they are just splendid to study, my class has just commenced to study both of them and we dont have books to study out of but study off of the black bord.

February 14, 1881. Today is valentine day, I dont know why but it is, and Maggie got a valentine and so did I get 1 and hers says To My Valentine and mine says To My Dear Love, and I like what mine says the most, an they have pitchures on them. Maggies has 2 birds and they look as if they are going to bite each other but Maggie says she guesses it means they are kissing and not biting, and mine has 2 hearts and a stick run through them to keep them together like the bucher fixes schewers in meat only the pitchure schewer is an arra.

February 21, and I am 9 years old today it is my
Birthday thats why, and tomorrow is George Wash-
ingtons Birthday only he is not living and I am.
He is to old to be living thats why, and tomorrow at
school my class has to make an essay about him,
an essay is when you write about things. I mean
each of us must write one apiece and we musent
copy it out of any history books and our Fathers
and our Mothers musent help us either and it
musent be longer than 130 words or shorter either,
and it must be personal, I asked Mamma how
to spell personal and what it means and this is
what I wrote, George Washington was tall and not
very good looking, he had large hands and a large
nose, any way they look big in the pitchures, When
he was 13 years old he made 110 rules for himself
to use to learn how to be polite and to behave well.
Maybe when I am 13 years old I will make some
too only I dont believe I will need so many. 25 or
30 will be enough I guess. He married Martha
Custis and she had been married once before and
had plenty of money. He died of laryngittis and

I have had it twice and never died yet. He went to the grave Childless that means he had no children, the only thing he was Father to was his country. Thats all I could write for it took all of my 130 words. Papa says there isent any doubt about its being personal enough. Its the first Essay I ever made and I like to make them very much.

March 1. 1881. It has snowed all day and it is just terrible cold and I have a bad sore throte so stayed home from school because my throte is sore. I wish it would come ½ past 4 oclock for I want Maggie to come home from school, I am tired of only me to play with. We are going to have chicken for supper and lots of good things and it smells good cooking and Mamma went over and asked old Elizabeth —— to come over and eat supper here, she is poor and likes chicken more than anything else so thats why, I made some poetry today and it is beautiful I think and so does Mamma think so too, here it is,

> Little Robin Red-breast
> Sing away with glee
> Go and build your nest
> Away up in a tree,

Then hatch your eggs of blue
Up in your nest so high
And soon your babies new
Will learn just how to fly.

My poetry I made March 1, 1881. Mary S. Paxson

March 2, 1881. My sore throte isent better so I couldent go to school again today. I have to study my lessons and Mamma hears them. Papa brought me some figs and dates and oranges because my throte is sore, I put half away for Maggie. Mamma says I am writing better but my spelling is poor. I wiped the breakfast dishes for Mattie today. I had my doll in her coach and left it stand near the fire and the heat made Beth look terrible. Beth is the only nice doll I have and now she is all spoiled and I dont know what to do. Meg and Jo don't look very good and Amy has had 1 new head and needs another for she fell on her face and cracked it and her nose got banged in, and Papa says she has seen her best days, and now Beth my best one of all is all ugly, I wish I had 10 nice new dolls.

March 4, 1881. I havent been to school any day this week, my sore throte is better and I am to stay in til Monday then go to school. I like lots of hollidays but I dont like to stay home from school and have sore throtes when it isent hollidays. Here are some words I must fix right, isn't, can't, evry. Papa says Garfield our new president is to be ennagurated today, he gets it done at Washington where he has to live because he was made a president thats why. Beths eyes fell in her head today and now I can't play with her ever again. I do want a doll so bad with real hair and shoes and stockings. Beth was wax and if she hadent been she would be nice yet. Anna and Meg and Jo look bad but I just can't play with Beth without eyes. She was my faverite.

March 12, Timmy has a cold and snezzes, he is getting old, he is 10 years old and that is a good while for a cat. He is 1 year older than I am.

March 14, 1881. Timmies cold is well. It is very cold weather. We went to school and when we came home before it was supper time we took our sleds and Rachie Preston went along and we coasted on the hill in the field back of our house and we had a splendid time.

March 24. 1881. I heard some birds sing this morning, and so did Mamma and Maggie. I love birds and I am going to make some more poetry about them when I get time. Papa and Mr. Woodruffs visited schools today, ours too. Mr. Woodruffs is our county supperintendent, he always stays at our house at nights when he visits schools near here and he calls Maggie and me cubs and we don't like to be called cubs.

April 29, 1881. Tilly Aunt made a party and Maggie and I went because she asked us to come, she is a grone woman but she asked all the school children and had a party for us and there werent any grone people asked, only just the school boys and girls that were little. We went to school all day and we were dressed better than we are evry day when there isn't to be a party and then when school was out we went to the party and had supper and we ate our suppers out doors and ate lots of good things and we played games and when it got dark we came home. Its the first party I ever went to and I like them and so does Maggie like them. Papa had a man to dig garden and we have peas and potatoes planted.

April 30th, 1881. Papa gave me a new doll because I worked a puzzle he said I couldent work thats why. It has wax hair and painted shoes. I do want a baby with real hair and real shoes but Ime very glad to have this one. I named her Eleanor after nobody. The first doll I ever had except my Katie rag doll came in my dolly bed and her name was Ruth and I named her for Mamma. She is a reck now. Maggie made my new doll a hat and I made her an apern and thats all the close she has yet except her painted shoes.

May 1st, 1881. It is pretty near summer time then it will be vacation. Uncle Howard Riches and Uncle Quimbys came here today for dinner, and a baby came at Pickerings today too. I wish 1 would come to our place.

May 7th, 1881. The most I have to say is we have a piano and Maggie and I began to learn to play it today for we took a music lesson apiece and its nice and we have to practice ½ hour evry day only not on Sundays. Mamma says that is long as we need practice while we go to school but when vacation comes we must do it one hour apiece, gracious.

May 15th 1881 We went down to Grandpa Paxsons to dinner today. Grandma had ginny for dinner.

We helped her carry the butter and things up out of the Spring house.

May 18th, 1881. Mr. Woodruffs came to visit our school today and came here to stay all night. He heard my arithametic class and he talks so loud he scares us. He played our piano after supper and sang some and he did it terrible loud and bangy.

May 28th, 1881. The big apple tree in Mrs. Waltons lane is full of flowers and Maggie and I got a lot, we reached out of our bed room window thats how.

May 30th, 1881. It is Decoration Day and whenever it is that day our school decorates the  solgiers graves, we only have to do it once evrey year. We wear badges and they are black silk made round like penwipers and 3 streemers hanging down and the streemers are red and white and blue ribbon and the badges look like this, there are a good many solgiers burried in our cemmetery. My father was a solgier once and Ime glad he diden't get killed or anything, some solgiers haven't any arms and legs when they get away from the war. I don't know what would have become of Maggie or me either if our Father had been killed, I guess nothing much for we werent born yet, and we had music and speaking pieces and some sollem things read out of a book and I had to speak a peice and evry body sang songs and a man prayed and what I liked the most was to march around the cemmetery all us school children and put piles and piles and piles of flowers on evry solgiers grave and there were enough to cover evry grave all over with big bokays of flowers.

June 1st, 1881. Today has been a school Reunion and it was at Soleberry Deer Park and all the schools in our township had to be there and Papa had to sit on the Platfrom with the school Directors because he is a school Director thats why. My geography class had to draw Maps and answer questions, and all the schools did a lot of things. I had to draw Maine evrey body in my geography class had to draw a different state and put all the cities where they ought to be and all the rivers and things where they belong and I made mine right, we had to remember how to draw them and daren't look in any geography book, we couldn't anyway because we hadent any books with us. It is bed time and school is out and that is all I have to say.

June 11th, 1881. It is Saturday, we helped Mamma and we took our music lessons and I was very busy in my play house while Maggie took her music lesson. I made a pie and it was a real pie and it was an apple pie and lots of sugar in it and Mamma baked it in the stove oven for me and it was very good. Maggie helped me eat it, Maggie would rather read than bake but I like to play house and cook. Maggie is going to be a Doctor when she is grone up and I am going to keep house and sew and cook but not wipe dishes.

July 2nd, 1881. I have a terrible happening to write about in my Diary, president Garfield was shot at 9 oclock this morning at the rail road station in Washington the place where he lived so he could be president but he wasent killed. A man did it on purpose, he is very wicked.

July 4th, 1881. There is no cellebration today because president Garfield was shot and is too sick for folks to make a holliday and have fire works and things thats why. I read my diary all threw today I wish our girl wiped dishes and so does Maggie.

July 9th, 1881. We got Under The Lilacs out of the librerry today and after we take naps and get washed and our clean close on Mamma is going to read it to us while we make our patchwork, I made Eleanor a new dress yesterday Mamma cut it out for me, and when I was dressing Eleanor up in it she fell to pieces, Mamma says she will get me a new doll with real hair I wish she would do it real soon. We practice on the piano 1 hour apiece evrey day and I think music lessons just splendid, and today when we went to the librerry to get a new book, it is in a room back of where Sammy Jones has a store and he said when we went home for us to ask Mamma if she remembered the day he missed a word in the spelling class at school and Mamma spelled it right he rememberred what word it was and for us to ask Mamma if she did and when we got home we asked Mamma and she told us all about it and she said she guest she did remember and she guest she would to her dyeing day, she said it was when she was a little girl and Sammy Jones was little too and

Mammas name was Ruth Shaw then and she hadent got to be our mother yet and she went to the old 8 Square School House and it was named that because it had 8 sides thats why, and Sammy Jones went there and so did Papa and Uncle Ben Shaw and Mamma was number 2 in the spelling class and Sammy Jones was number 1 and had been up head all Winter and one day he missed a word and Mamma spelled it right and went up head and the word was psalter and Sammy Jones spelled it salter and I guess I would too mebby, and the next time we go to the librerry to get a book we are going to tell him she did remember all about it and what the word was and evrey thing.

July 11th, 1881 Papa went fishing today and caught 6 bass and 1 elle, I don't like fish to eat.

August 18th, 1881. Today is my fathers birthday and he is 40 years old It is very hot wether this summer and president Garfield is so sick because he was shot on purpose and he can never get well again. Mamma is going to take Maggie and me to the seashore tomorrow, it will be just splendid and we can hardly wait and we wish Papa could go along but he says he cant spare a whole week to go to the sea shore in but mebby he will come

down a day or 2. Maggie has 2 new dresses and
so have I 2.

August 22, 1881, On last Friday we left papa all
alone with Timmy and he was 40 years old on his
birthday and Mamma and Maggie and I went to
Alantic City. We had a good time evrey day all
day long and dident have to take any naps all
the time we were there, and just had a splendid
time all but my splinter and mosquittoes. We
stayed at the same Hotel where we stayed 2 years
ago but we only stayed 1 week this time, we
wisht we could stay 2 weeks now for we dident
get done. Maggie and I took our buckets and
shovels along, we got them at Alantic City 2
years ago and played in the sand and in the ocean
all we wanted too and that was all the time evrey
day, and there was a reck washed up on the beech,
a reck is a boat all banged to peaces. It used to be
a big boat and we played in one end of it all we
wanted too and we had a splendid time being ship
recked, Maggie and I and 2 boys we found. We
couldent play in one end of the reck because that
end stuck out in the ocean and a man told us that
we musent play in that end. He said we might play
in the other end all we wanted to and we did so, and

we wisht we could stay 2
weeks now for we dident get
done.

one boys name was Guy and the other was Charlie
and there Mothers name was Mrs. Channing and
our Mother sat with their Mother on the on the
beach and sewed and talked and we played and
we all bathed in the sea when 11 oclock came my
we had a splendid time, One day I was barefooted
and walked right into a big splinter it went away
into my foot and nearly made me cry it hurt so
but I dident and Mamma couldent get it out and
she dident know what to do and just then 2 young
men walked by and saw us and stopped and
offerred to help and one man cut it out with his
knife and it hurt awful but not so bad as when
the splinter was in my foot but I dident squeal and
I was lame all the rest of the time and one young
man told me I was a brave little girl because I
dident make any fuss thats why.

August 28th, 1881. We have piles and piles of
splendid peaches, and it is terribly hot wether, its
been the hottest summer that ever was thats
what the news papers say and poor shot president
Garfield has had to stay in bed all summer because
they shot him and it was hot in Washington where
he has to live when he is president, evrey president
has to live in Washington in a house called the

White House thats why, and they took president Garfield to a seashore place named Long Branch, and mebby now the place where he got shot will get well and mebby not. The wicked man that shot him on purpose was Gitteau, I don't know why he did it. It was 106° in the shade today. I hemmed 2 towels today and Maggie did too. We both have new shoes to start to school with and new aperns and each of us a new slate and new slate pencils and new sponges. We practice evrey day and read and play and sew our patch work blocks and help Mamma, and we made bows and arrows and the first thing I did when I shot my arrows was to brake a window pane, because my arrow went the wrong way. Mamma says its the safest to shoot right up in the air and thats just what I was doing when the window got smashed.

September 10th, 1881. The Thermommeter says it is 108 and it hangs in the shade and papa said holey smokes he hopes it wont get much hotter. It is terribly hot to go to school. I study lots of things, reading, spelling definitions tables geography mental arithmetic history tables and we study literature off of the black bord and when poets get born and what poems I like everything

I study but mental arithmetic and this is the very first time I ever spelled every right

September 1881. There was a great fire in mishigen and it was very far away and mamma is very busey making things, petty kotes and night panties and dresses and things to send in barrells where the fire burned every thing up and a great many people and children and babies and other folks havent any close and Maggie and I help sew and Grace Shaw and Alice Wothingdon came and helped mamma and we are very busey. I had to take a page out the back of my diary because I forgot to write it when it was.

September 12, 1881 it is not really Monday but I forgot to write there was a arora bory alice tonight and I never saw any thing so beautyfull.

September 18 It is Sunday and we went to Uncle Howard Riches to dinner and Grandfather S——— is very sick, I dont like him very much, and Maggie doesn't either. He isn't our real Grandfather, he is just a step one. He married our Grandmother Shaw after our real Grandfather died, that was a good many years ago before my time and Maggies either. Mamma was only 1 year old when he died,

he was her real father, this one is her step same as
he is our step.

September 20th, 1881. There is a very sad thing
to write about, because president Garfield didn't
get well at all, he died at the seashore where they
took him, he died last night. He ought not to have
been shot it was a very wicked thing to do.

September 24th, 1881. It is Saturday and I have
lots to write about. Aunt Ann Good is here making
us a visit, she is my Mothers Aunt and lives in
Delaware and she says I sew very well for 9
years old to do. I have my patch work quilt most
done, and so has Maggie hers. I sewed all the blocks
all myself but Grandmother Scarborough helped
me sew some long seams when I put it together
but she is not living now so I guess noboddy will
help me. Some of the seams in the middle are very
long. Mamma is making us new school aprons,
they are gingham Mother Hubbard ones and have
long sleeves just like our old ones. I wore my old
ones all summer in the mornings for dresses It
was so hot and they look like dresses and were
cooler than dresses thats why. Mamma is making
each of us 2 white ones for best, and they haven't

sleeves like the school ones only a ruffel around the arm holes and necks.

October 1st, 1881. We went to the dentists today.

November 3rd, 1881. It is Institute week and we haven't any school. Today is Fifth day and last Seventh day Mamma and Papa and Maggie and I went to pay Uncle Will Walters a visit, we had a splendid time and Maggie and I wanted to stay there with Horace and Elliott instead of going to Cousin David Wilsons to pay another visit and it rained all the time we visited at Wilsons and we couldn't do anything out doors and I was glad to get back home to Timmy and he was glad to see us. We are going to do something splendid this after noon, we are going to Winfields wedding I will write about it tomorrow, we have to go to the Church at 3 oclock to see them get married thats why.

November 4th, 1881 Win and Hannah were married yesterday in the Presbiterrian Church and we went and it rained in torrints, we went to the receptshion in the evening and it was terribly rainy. We had a good time and evreybody had lots of good supper and cake and things. Papa went gunning today and brought home 3 little dead rabbits, poor little dead bunnies they cant run around in the woods and have a good time any more.

November 5th, 1881. Our vacation week is most over.

December 3rd, 1881 Our new piano came today, the one we have had was rented and it didn't belong to us and it went back to Cowdricks because it belonged to them thats why. Our sitting room is pretty full of things Mamma says when Maggie and I get a little bigger she is going to turn our play room into a parlor and put our piano there

December 11th, 1881. It is Sunday and we went to Uncle Wilsons to dinner and Grandma and Grandpa Paxson were there, they are all the grandfathers and grandmothers we have. Last night we went to an oyster supper at Uncle Eds and there were a lot of people there and I got terribly hungry before I got any supper. Most alwes big people alwes eat first thats why.

December 13 My father and Uncle Billy Morris visited our school today they are school directers thats why.

1882

February 21st 1882 Its been a new year a long time and I havent written in my Diary for weeks and weeks and weeks because I hadn't much to say thats why, I am 10 years old today and mamma gave me a book and papa gave me candy and Maggie gave me 2 hankerchiefs in a nice box and Win and Hanna gave me some pictures. I like Birthdays. My Grandma Paxson can't have a Birthday very often, her Birthday comes on February 29th and there isn't any only every 4 years when it is leap year. Its very queer.

February 25th Maggie and I went to the store today and got candies. Mine was a red solgier toy candy and so was Maggies and I named mine Ben Shaw he was my Uncle and Maggie named hers Abrum Linkum and he was a president one time and he was shot too just like president Garfield was, and we had to change the names of our candy men because I didn't want to eat my Uncle and Maggie didn't want to eat Mr. Abrum Linkum so she named her solgier Jeffersin Davis and I named mine Benny Dick Arnuld 2 men that ought to be eat and we ate them up heads first.

March 6th. 1882 Mamma went to Philadelphia and brought me a doll and its the best and nicest thing I have to write about for ever so long. Ive wanted one just exactly like it a grate while. It has real hair and it is curly and short and I can brush and comb it and not have to make believe its hair for it is, I can wash my new doll all over, she has dear little toes and Mamma brought me 2 pairs of real shoes for her, one pair of pink shoes and one pair of brown slippers They are the nicest presents I ever owned and it isn't Christmas or Birthdays or nothing. I named my new doll Winifred.

March 25, 1882 Yesterday Longfellow died, he lived in Cambridge and for our literature lesson at school tomorrow we have to learn about his life and my class has a poem to learn that he made, he made several. I studied about his life and learned the old clock on the stair, Mamma heard me say them both and I don't know the poem very well yet. Maggie has to learn Evangeline and we must both study them more before bed time, we dont have to learn but 2 verses of the poems but Maggie

Mamma brought me a doll and its the best and nicest thing I have to write about for ever so long

learned 3 I didnt. We had shad for supper tonight and Papa said it was good only I dont like fish to eat.

June 27th, 1882. It has been a long time since I wrote in my Diary. I got dinner all myself today. Mamma and Maggie went to Philadelphia today and I made the beds and wiped and washed the breakfast dishes. I played with Winifred some and washed some of her clothes. I am very fond of her. Aunt Ellie says I am a big girl to play with dolls, but I don't think 10 years old is too big. I do lots of other things. Grandma Paxson came up to be here today but Uncle Jesse —— is so sick so she went over to help Aunt Annie, so I got our dinner and papa says it was all right. Aunt Annie Black is Grandmas sister just like Maggie is my sister.

July 4th, 1882 Uncle Jesse died last Wednesday and he was burried on July 2 and Aunt Priscilla Small is here for a visit. We had fire crackers and tor-pidose today and fire works this evening. Last year nobody had any because Garfield was shot. Giteau the wicked man that shot him was hanged in Washington last Saturday served him right. Mat-tie came back because her vacaticon was over.

She works for Mamma but Maggie and I have to wipe dishes.

July 6th, 1882 Papa is away, he went to see Uncle Will Walter, he is very sick, Uncle Joseph was going with papa they went yesterday and last night Maggie and I both slept with Mamma and this morning we found Timmy all curled up in the middle of our bed where he was all night. Maggie and I have a duet to learn, a duet is where 2 people play both at once. I made some more poetry today and I put it in the back of my Diary with my other poetry.

July 20th, 1882 It is hot. I put Winifreds hammock in our cherry tree and its nice out there. Maggie and I have a milliner shop in the chery tree, we make hats and bonnets out of leaves and pin the leaves fast to other ones with pins that we make out of stems and we pin flowers on our hats that way. My doll hammock is bran new, I made it myself out of mack raymay, Aunt Ada showed me the way to make it. She was here to pay us a visit and Emma too and Emma brought her doll Hellen, Nelly for short and we had a splendid time. We traded doll night gounds because she liked my dolls night gound better than Nellies and I liked

Nellies better than Winifreds thats why. We had
school for our dolls

August 28th 1882 I had 3 teeth filled at the
Dentists.

September 10th, 1882. More school and vacation
is all over for a whole year. I like school now because I don't have to study mental arithmetic any
more. Old Jonathan —— died yesterday, he wont
get drunk any more I guess. Uncle Quimbys and
Uncle Eds and John Gilberts were to our house to
eat dinner today. The things I like is having company and going to the matinee and dolls and cats
and my Mother and my Father and Maggie and
good times and what I don't like is going to the
dentist and mental arithmetic and warts, lots of
the boys at school have warts and I cant bare to
take hold of their hands when we play games, it
is my bed time.

October 4th 1882 Mamma and Papa went to the
Fair at Doylestown and Maggie and I went went
to school and we came home and said lets have
supper all ready when they get home and we
have it all ready and are waiting for them to come
home. Mattie is home sick.

October 7th, 1882. Mamma brought me a balloon when she came home from the Fair and Maggie I too and we tied our little stuffed pigs to the end of the strings and when the balloons rose up the pigs went too and it looked awfully funny, we had lots of fun, but the balloons just all shrunk up to little bits of ones in a day and the stuff inside didn't swell them out any more. Today is Maggies Birthday and she is 12 years old and we went down to Grandpas and hunted chestnuts and found lots and lots and Grandpa gave us lots more than we found. We are going to have apples and boiled chestnuts now and it is pretty near bed time only we don't have to go to bed til we have eaten them.

October 8th, 1882 We went to Meeting this morning and last First day we went to Plumstead Meeting.

October 19th, 1882. This is Institute Week and we havent any school. I don't know what to do for Maggie likes to read better than play, she doesn't play with dolls any more and I do, any I want someboddy to play with. I wish I had a twin sister just my age so we could play with dolls lots.

November 1st, 1882 Mamma read us Faith Gartneys Girlhood and I like what I do the best only

I don't do many new things. I wish I knew if you walked off of the earth right straight and kept on going how soon you would come around to the earth again, but maybe the outside isn't round but just straight ahead miles and miles out, and I wish I knew why the world don't turn round from east to west instead of the other way.

November 27th, 1882 Mamma is 41 years old today. Papa gave her a gold watch chain and Maggie croshayed her some lace for an apron and I made her 2 holders and a pin cushion. Not this year but 1 time every 7 years Mammas Birthday comes on Thanksgiving Day.

November 30th, 1882 We didn't have any school today because it is Thanksgiving Day thats why, and Uncle Quimbys and Grandma were here to dinner and we had 2 roasted ducks and lots of good things. It is sleighing and we took Grandma home in the sleigh tonight. My it was nice.

We didnt want supper because we were too full of dinner thats why. There is always lots to eat I love to go sleigh in the Winter time and nights and so does Maggie only we don't very often go at night. Tomorrow at school we must tell 3 things we are thankful for, I mean each one must tell 3 things apiece, and I am thankful once that I havent any warts, and thankful twice that we have plenty of things to eat and thankful three times that I have a Mother and a Father and a Sister and a cat and six dolls and many more things.

December 27th, 1882 Mamma and Papa went to Willie Quimbies wedding today, he is getting married to Catharine Johnson, Maggie and I did not go because we were not asked thats why. We are asked to the reception at Uncle Quimbies on Saturday evening and Mamma says we are to go. We have new dresses and so has Mamma only hers is silk and ours aren't. My new dress is red. Maggie and I have a very beautiful Christmas tree. I got 2 bottles of colone and so did Maggie and a new game and I got little cups and saucers, Mamma gave me 1 and the Quimby girls gave me 1 too, and Hanna gave my doll Winifred a beautiful coat and cap and they are pink and Win gave her new stuff to make a pink dress out of and pink buttons because she is named for him, his name is Winfield but she has to be named Winifred because she is a girl thats why. Mamma and Papa gave us each a book and I have a new game too and each of us a new collar and hair ribbons and gloves for

Maggie and I have a very beautiful
Christmas tree.

best and mittens for school and oranges and nuts
and candies and things.

December 31, 1882. Maggie and I made a lot of old
ladies, we made them out of shellbarks for heads
and dressed them all and we made a house for them
to live in and we fixed cotton all on top of the house
for snow and had snow every where and it was
beautiful and we put our little red Christmas
candles in the windows and we were going to light
them and we we were going to have tabblelows and
it was to be a surprise to Mamma and what we did
was to burn it all up, old ladies and everything. It
was to be called an Old Ladies Home and when we
lit the candles everything caught fire and I guess
it was a good thing Mamma was there for she put
the fire out. It burned a big hole in a chair where
we had the house. I was scared and so was Maggie
scared.

1883

January 1st, 1883 I don't know what to say but it is a new year and today is a New Years day, and I am going to write a story and call my story The Charity Pupil, I guess I will write it now because I haven't anybody to play with because Maggie would rather read than play.

January 10th, 1883 I have a bad cold and havent been to school yesterday and today, Mamma hears my lessons I got my story made and Mamma read it and she says it is very nice.

Uncle Will Walter died on the 2nd of January. Papa went down right away, he died of consumption. I wish I didnt have to wipe dishes for Mattie but Mamma says we must learn to be cape able. I'de just as lieve not and so would Maggie.

February 21st, 1883 I am 11 years old today and I was to be in an entertament at the Hillside but I have a very bad sore throte. I learned my part but Katie Hocomb is to be it instead of me, she is coming here to stay all night and I wish I could go because I like to take part in entertaments and I am so much disappointed I dont know what I shall do. Our school is raising money to buy a solgiers monument and Mr Evans is making this entertament to make money to buy the monument thats why. It is to be tomorrow night.

February 22nd, 1883 I feel so bad because I am not well enough to go tonight but my throte is very sore and Mamma says no. What I was to do if I hadn't a mean sore throte is to be dressed all in a white dress and my curls all hanging loose around my head and I was to be called the white child of the world welkoming the children of all Nations and they were Japanneze and yellow and Indians and red and Eskimose and little black ones I guess Africans and lots others. Katie Hocomb came home from school with Maggie and she is going to wear my white dress and all my things Mamma fixed for me to wear tonight. Today at school we had things in History Class about George Washington because it is his birthday thats why. I couldnt go to school but Maggie took my paper that I fixed. The teacher fixed his name this way

G   on a piece of paper
E   and my History Class
O   must find a
R   word for each
G   letter that
E   means something
W   George Washington is,
A   and we dare look
S   in our History
H   Books all we want
I   but we mustn't
N   have any help.
G   These are
T   the words I
O   fixed his
N   name with,

G eneral   W ar
E nglish   A rmy
O fficer   S oldiers
R ebellion   H istory
G overnment   I ndian
E poch   N egotiated
                  G uns
                  T ories
                  O ath of office   3 ose
                  N ation

I got every word out of my History Book.

My class at school has money jugs and only little slits to put money in and no place to get it out. We are colleckting money that way for our Soldiers monument and after the entertament is done the jugs are going to be broken open and our money counted, oh I wish I could be there so bad.

February 23rd, 1883 My jug had more in it that any other jug, it had 4 dollars and 60 cents in it. Maggie and Katie have gone to school and my sore throte is named tonsillitis and is very sore.

February 28th, 1883 Grandma was 68 years old today and she had a Birthday party and we had a splendid time, and there were 60 people there. Mamma gave her a new table cloth and Papa gave her lots of new black alpacka to make a new dress out of. Grandma doesnt really have any birthdays only when it is February 29 because that is her real Birthday and it comes in Leap Year and never any other time, so when it isn't Leap Year she has her Birthday on February 28th.

March 6th, 1883 I have a beautiful ring and its the only ring I ever had and I bought it with my own money. It is an amethist ring and that is my birthday stone only I couldn't get my new ring

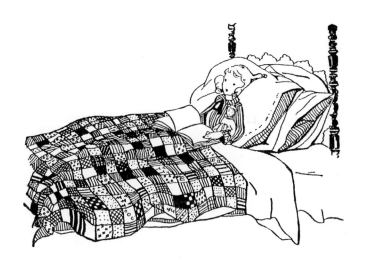

my sore throte is named tonsillitis
and is very sore.

for my birthday because I hadn't saved enough money then. I hemmed a towel and Mamma read Helens Babies to us, it is funny and when we get our kittens we are going to name them Budge and Toddie

June 18th, 1883 I dont do much to write about, the barn at the Hillside burned today. I like to look at fires but they are terrible things to have. I read and play and help Mamma and take naps and take music lessons and practice. I wish something just lovely would happen.

June 22nd, 1883 I wish I never had to work or sew or study or practice or anything but take my doll and my cat and go in the woods and pick flowers and wade and be happy and never be scolded any more, Papa scolded me because he says I am careless.

July 1st, 1883. We went to First Day School and Meeting and to Grandmas to dinner. I took Winifred along but nobody knew it til we got to Grandmas. I wore my blue silk dress and so did Maggie we wear dresses alike.

July 10th, 1883 Maggie and I have a new play house on the upper porch. I make lots of real things to eat and if they arent good to eat raw Mamma lets me cook them on her real stove. Maggie helps me eat what I cook.

I dont know what to do so I guess I'll make some poetry.

> I make pies and cakes
> And these Mamma bakes
> And she says mercy sakes
> What a short time it takes.

She means mercy sakes it doesn't take long for little things to get done in the stove oven thats why.

July 15th, 1883 We had a siclone today and it did lots of damage. It came up our street and things look awful. Papa wrote all about it in his Diary. A siclone is lots and piles of wind and it blows terribly.

July 30th, 1883 I made a sunbonnet for Winifred today. I rubbed what I wrote out because Mamma says it isnt graceious to say ugly things about people but I dont mind, my Mothers Aunt ——, she is not my aunt but my great, is visiting us and she said I am to old to play with dolls and no girl ought to have 7 enny way and I ought to sew more because I sew poor and I heard my Mother say to my father that Aunt —— judgses from to mattuer eyes for Janey thats me sews very well for a child of 11 years and she hopes I will play with dolls for many years yet and Papa said Ruth something but I couldent hear the rest of what Papa told Mamma.

August 6, 1883. Aunt —— went home to Wilmington in Delaware today and Maggie and I can do a lot more things now. She is osteer papa says.

September 9, 1883. Mamma read Enoch Arden out loud to us. I had to copy how to spell it. Mamma says she wants us to like good reading. We have a great many books and we learn some verses 1 time every week. Verses are named poetry or the other way about I forget which and Mamma has gone to see Grace Shaw this afternoon so I cant ask and Maggie says what differents does it make. We are home from school and have changed our school shoes for scarry fide old ones like we have to do and then we can climb trees and see saw and roller scate and jump rope and not spoil our nice shoes. Every summer since we been old enough to wear shoes we go to the shoemakers and he masures our stocking feet and makes us

2 pears, I mean he makes each of us 2 pears apiece one of mo rock a lether and one out of calf skin and the calf skin lether ones are to go to school in and the mo rock a ones are our very best ones. We are going to take our spelling books and clime the apple tree and hear our spelling lessons.

September 18th 1883 My mother has some very beautyfull roses and I helped her work in the garden. A man works in the garden where we have things to eat. Our girl cant cook things as good as Mamma does. Papa says he could tell the difference with both eyes shut.

November 9th, 1883 My father visited our school today and made a speech and so did Mr. Woodruff, he is our Supperintent and he heard my spelling class and gave us some hard words and some easy ones and we had calfes liver for supper and corn bread and baked potatoes and the last of our lima beans and cold slaugh and for the last we had peaches and sponge cake and piles of cream and the very best water pitcher and gobblets.

November 28th It is my mothers birthday and she 41 years old today and Maggie gave her a glass dish and I made her 2 holders and papa gave her a book and a table cloth because it is her birthday.

December 1883 It is Christmas day and Papa has presents, and so has Mamma and the nicest and most Maggie and I got is gold chains for our necks with little gold crosses hanging on them. We have a Christmas tree and lots and piles of things. I gave 2 of my dolls away.

1884

January 1st 1884 Mamma and Papa went to Philadellphia today and are not coming home for a long time and we had fried potatoes for supper and Martha Jane made them so greasy Maggie and I couldnt eat them and she got very cross at us. I am going to make some poetry.

> Martha Jane is bony and big
> And cooks things in pans of grease
> And Maggie and I dont care a fig
> If she is mad and we have no peace,
> For we can't eat greasy things she cooks
> And we don't like her anyway
> We don't like her meals and her looks
> And we don't like what she say.
>   her scold say

January 4th 1884. Mamma and Papa came home today. I wish they would never go away, and so does Maggie wish so. The boys at school put me through the hole where a pane was out in the windows that are between the school room and the vesta buel and I'm skinny so I went through easy. Maggie and I went on the hill with our sleds and it was sleet and we sled down hill easier than we could walk up.

January 10th 1884 I cut out some pages out of my diary to do puzzles on and now I havent many more leaves to fill. Maggie and I wanted some paper to work puzzles on and Mamma was not home to give us any, we work lots of puzzles out of Scattered Seeds and Maggie made 2 and they were in it, so I took some leaves out of my diary.

February 21. 1884 I am 12 years old today and my mother and father gave me a watch and fob and I am very happy. It isn't Maggies birthday but she has a watch too for Mamma said she doesn't want to show partiality. I have more birthday presents. Maggie gave me a book and Winfield and Hannah gave me some figs and a box to put my handkerchiefs in when they are clean. I have 9. Maggie has 13. Mamma says I am not to wear curls any longer but am to have my hair cut short. I don't believe I will write another diary because I have no book and I dont do much to write about.

Maggie and I roller skate a lot. On rainy days

On rainy days we skate up garret and
Mamma says what a racket

we skate up garret and Mamma says what a racket and sometimes we go to the skating rink and we have 3 big porches to skate on.

March 2, 1884 Mamma went to Philadelphia and Maggie and I went too and we had lunch at a place called Part Riges and after Mamma bought each of us new spring coats and one for her self we went to a matinee and it was Pinafore and very beautiful and then we went to a hotel called Bingham House and Papa was there waiting for us and our Mother and Father let Maggie and me say just exactly what we wanted to have to eat off of a Bill Of Fare and we said lots of good things. We were there all night and for breakfast and we came home this afternoon. I haven't any more pages because I tore them out because I needed paper once and I guess I wont write any more diary's.

Good bye.

Oddments

July 10th, 1881. Mamma made me some poetry and here it is and it is verry beautifull I think, so I copied it.

Blue bird where did you get the paint that makes
     your feathers so blue?
I flew up high and I touched the sky, thats where
     I got my hue.

> Little Robin Red Breast,
> Sing away with glee
> Go and build your nest
> Away up in a tree.
>
> Then hatch your eggs of blue
> Up in your nest so high
> And soon your babies new
> Will learn just how to fly.

My Poetry I made March 1, 1881 Mary S Paxson

Some more poetry I made July 6th, 1882,
Things I like and dont.
I like books and babies and dolls and cats
But not wasps and snakes and worms and bats.

I like birds and turtles and flowers and trees
But not warts and freckles and poison and fleas.
Mary S Paxson   Carversville

My Mother's Work Basket.

My Mother's work basket is very full
Of scissors and thread and pieces of wool,
Emmery and wax and a tape masure too
Some things are old and some things are new.

Her workbasket is full for she needs the things
When she sews and mends and patches and sings
And she makes aprons and things out of new stuff
I guess I've made my poem long enough

My poetry I made January 1st, 1883.

I was named for Mary Small and Mary Scarborough and Mamma just put S in the Bible and
she says when I am old enough to choose I can say
which is my middle name, and I'm going to choose
Scarborough.

THE CHARITY PUPIL

My Story I Made January 1st, 1883.

Mary S. Paxson.

Chapter 1. The Charity Pupil. Miss Maggie Brown had red hair and freckles and her nose nose went up and she had a great many brains and she wasn't very good looking. She was very nice and when people are very nice they dont have to be very good looking because other people like them any way. She was tall and sort of bony and lived with her Uncle Ben. He was a real old man and would be forty years old on his next Birthday. And Miss Maggie wasn't so old yet, she would be twenty five on her next Birthday, and she said one day to her Uncle Ben lets both of us start a school and have girls come to it and learn lots of things they otta know and her Uncle Ben said Maggie why dont you want to teach boys to learn a lot of things too and Maggie said she didn't know why she didn't, and her Uncle Ben said he was a boy once and didn't care much whether he learned a lot of things at school or not, and they said if that was the case they would have nobody but girls and thats the reason there were only girls at the Charity School, and a sign was nailed up on the School House gate post like this, A School For Girls and no boys need come.

Chapter 2. And one day when Miss Maggie Brown and her Uncle Ben and the negro colored man were getting lots of desks and things fixed in what used to be the parlor but wasn't to be now because it was to be a school room, Maggie said Uncle Ben I had a letter from Uncle David and he says we can have one girl come to our school and learn things and he is rich and will pay for her and we must pick out a girl that is poor enough so she couldn't come to school if somebody didn't pay for her to learn, so we will tell folks that we will have one pupil that we have a fund for to edducate with and so she wont have to pay and all the other ones that come to school will have to pay us, and that is the way it was fixed.

Chapter 3. Then one day 12 girls came to school and nobody was to be told which one the Charity Pupil was because sometimes Charity people get treated mean and not fair. One girl with long black curls and no very nice dresses and only one hair ribbon was called Ruth Shaw and because she didn't have but one best dress and gingham aprons instead of white ones like the 11 other ones wore, the 11 other ones said she was it and they got so as they didn't act any too nice to her because she was Charity.

Chapter 4. And one day Maggie's Uncle Ben said to her Maggie this wont do, I'm not going to have Ruth treated nasty any more days lets tell them the truth, and the next day Miss Maggie said girls I have something very important to say to you and what most of you deserve is to be spanked but mebby you will be ashamed enough and that may last longer than spanks. After my Uncle Ben and I commenced to have our school my Uncle Ben got a great pile of money left to him, just piles and heaps of it and we didn't have to work to earn money to get a new roof on our house and a new pump too but we said we would just go on any way because we wanted something to do even if we were not poor any more and the Minister said it was a worthey undertaking so when all your Mothers and Fathers all excepting Ruth's Mother and Father asked for you to be the free pupil we decided to take you all as Charities and charge only for Ruth because her folks are rich, and she is the only pay pupil in this school and you have all acted very unkind and unladylike to Ruth, and 1 by 1 you can tell Ruth you are ashamed and then we will proceed with our arithmetic lesson.

Chapter 5. And 1 by 1 the 11 Charities marched up to where Ruth's desk was and said they were ashamed, and then they all went to the blackboard and wrote the 12 times table up to 12 times 12.